Why Science Matters

Generating and Using Electricity

Andrew Solway

www.heinemann.co.uk/library
Visit our website to find out more information about **Heinemann Library** books.

To order:

 Phone 44 (0) 1865 888066

 Send a fax to 44 (0) 1865 314091

 Visit the Heinemann Bookshop at www.heinemann.co.uk/library to browse our catalogue and order online.

Heinemann Library is an imprint of Capstone Global Library Limited, a company incorporated in England and Wales having its registered office at 7 Pilgrim Street, London, EC4V 6LB – Registered company number: 6695582

"Heinemann" is a registered trademark of Pearson Education Limited, under licence to Capstone Global Library Limited

Edited by Pollyanna Poulter and Rebecca Vickers
Designed by Steven Mead and Q2A Creative Solutions
Original illustrations © Capstone Global Library Limited by
    Gordon Hurden and Kerry Flaherty
Picture research by Ruth Blair
Production by Victoria Fitzgerald
Originated by Heinemann Library
Printed and bound in China by Leo Paper Group.

ISBN 978 0 431040 92 9 (hardback)
13 12 11 10 09
10 9 8 7 6 5 4 3 2 1

British Library Cataloguing-in-Publication Data
Solway, Andrew
Generating and using electricity. - (Why science matters)
1. Electric power production - Juvenile literature
2. Electric power consumption - Juvenile literature
I. Title
621.3'1
A full catalogue record for this book is available from the British Library.

Acknowledgements
We would like to thank the following for permission to reproduce photographs: © Alamy pp. **5** (Deco), **22** (Michael Ventura), **41** (David J. Green – technology); © Corbis pp. **4** (Bettmann), **15** (John Gress/Reuters and with permission © A.M.P.A.S.®), **28** (Oswald Eckstein/Zefa), **40** (Tara Todras-Whitehill/Reuters), **47** (Pallava Bagla); © Getty Images pp. **6** (Stone), **18** (Justin Sullivan), **23** (Fabrice Coffrini/AFP), **43** (Yoshikazu Tsuno/AFP); © iStockphoto pp. **38** (Nathan Gutshall-Kresge), background images and design features; © NASA p. **33** (NASA Marshall Space Flight Center (NASA-MSFC)); © Newscast p. **34**; © Panasonic Corporation p. **21**; © PA Photos p. **39** (AP); © Peter Gould p. **13**; © Photolibrary Group pp. **20**, **31**, **32**, **42**; © Science & Society p. **14** (Science Museum); © Science Photo Library pp. **7** (Martyn F. Chillmaid), **8** (Peter Menzel), **11** (Robert Brook), **16** (Living Art Enterprises, LLC), **17** (Martin Bond), **25** (Andrew Lambert Photography), **36** (Jerry Mason).

Cover photograph of the view from Sears Tower, Chicago, at night reproduced with permission of © Alamy/Stephen Finn.

We would like to thank John Pucek for his invaluable help in the preparation of this book.

Every effort has been made to contact copyright holders of material reproduced in this book. Any omissions will be rectified in subsequent printings if notice is given to the Publishers.

Disclaimer
All the Internet addresses (URLs) given in this book were valid at the time of going to press. However, due to the dynamic nature of the Internet, some addresses may have changed, or sites may have changed or ceased to exist since publication. While the author and Publishers regret any inconvenience this may cause readers, no responsibility for any such changes can be accepted by either the author or the Publishers.

Contents

Some words are printed in bold, **like this**. You can find out what they mean in the glossary.

Electricity matters

There is no doubt that electricity matters. Without it our society cannot work. On 14th August 2003, a huge power blackout hit the northeast USA and parts of Canada. It was the largest power cut ever seen in North America. From about 4:00 p.m. until early the next morning, there was chaos. Offices, factories, and shops closed. Roads were gridlocked because traffic lights did not work. No trains were running so thousands of people walked for hours to get home, while those who couldn't slept outside. In places there was no tap water because the water pumps failed. The lives of 50 million people were affected and it took several days for things to return to normal.

This early power station was built by George Westinghouse, who was a rival manufacturer to Thomas Edison.

SCIENCE IN YOUR HOME: THINK ELECTRIC

Go around your house, look in every room, and count how many things use electricity. Don't forget things, such as torches, that use batteries rather than the mains. If you have central heating, the pump that moves the warm water or air through the system runs on electricity, and so does the timer. How many electrical devices does your family have in total? If you do the same thing at school, you will probably find an even larger number of electrical devices.

The spread of electricity

One of the places hit by the 2003 power cut was New York. Years earlier, in 1882, a small group of New Yorkers were among the very first people to get electric power. This was when Thomas Edison opened Pearl Street power station. It was one of the first power stations in the world. The six **dynamos** provided about 600 kW of power, enough to power Edison's new electric lights over about two square kilometres of Manhattan.

From this small beginning, electric power has grown and spread incredibly quickly. Today, we produce so much electricity that at night, the lights of cities and towns can be seen from space! Large, modern power stations produce 3,000 times as much power as Pearl Street. A network of millions of kilometres of cables carries electricity from power stations to all but the most remote areas.

The huge impact that electric lighting has had is clear in this view of Earth from space at night.

Electricity has made such a huge difference to our lives that it is almost impossible to imagine what life was like before it. We rely on electricity for everything, from keeping watches and clocks ticking to powering **atom**-smashing research in physics. Electricity is a very convenient form of energy. It works at the flick of a switch and can be turned into many other kinds of energy – for example heat, light, sound, or movement. This book will look at how we produce the vast amounts of electricity we use, and how it gets from where it is made to where it is needed. It also looks at the problems with the ways we generate electricity, and how we might avoid these problems in the future.

Charge!

Have you ever wondered how car manufacturers manage to give their cars such a smooth, shiny paint job? The cars are spray-painted. But if you have ever tried using spray paint, you will know that it is really hard to get an even coating. The secret to a car's glossy finish is actually static electricity.

Robots spray cars on a production line. The spraying process relies on static electricity to get a smooth, even coat (see page 10).

What is static electricity?

Static electricity is the build-up of electric charge on an object or material. You can see this in action by rubbing a balloon on your sweater and then sticking it to a wall. When you rub the balloon on your sweater, some of the **electrons** on the surface of it rub off and stick to the balloon. Electrons have a negative electric charge, so the balloon becomes negatively charged (because it has extra electrons) and the sweater becomes positively charged (because it has too few electrons). If something is negatively charged, it will be attracted to something positively charged, or with no overall charge. The wall has no overall charge, so the balloon is attracted to it and sticks.

If two things have the same electrostatic charge, they will repel (push against) each other rather than be attracted to each other. You can see this if you hang two balloons close to each other on pieces of thread. Once they are hung up, rub each balloon on your sweater. Both balloons will become negatively charged, and when they are hanging again, they will push away from each other.

A stream of running water has a slight positive electric charge. A negatively charged plastic rod will attract the stream of water, causing it to bend.

THE SCIENCE YOU LEARN: ELECTRICAL CHARGES

The electric charges involved in static electricity come from bits of atoms. Every atom has a nucleus containing particles called protons, which have a positive electrical charge. Around the nucleus there is a cloud of electrons, with a negative electric charge. An atom has the same number of protons as it has electrons, so overall it has no charge.

Unlike (different) electrical charges attract each other, whereas like (similar) electrical charges repel. Something with a positive charge will attract something negatively charged, but repel something positively charged.

These two Van de Graaff generators are in the Franklin Institute in Philadelphia, USA. They produce huge electric sparks. The metal cage below them is called a Faraday cage and protects the person inside it from the static discharge.

Static history

People have known about static electricity for thousands of years. Thales of Miletus, who lived about 2,600 years ago, knew that if **amber** was rubbed with a silk cloth it could pick up light objects, such as feathers.

Static electricity was just a curiosity until the 17th century, when scientists in Europe began to study it. As they learned more, they developed ways of creating large, static electricity charges, and also ways to store the charge. An early device for producing charge was a ball of sulfur that rotated on a shaft. Rubbing the ball as it rotated created an electrostatic charge. German scientist and inventor, Otto von Guericke, built this simple "electrostatic machine" in about 1660.

In the 18th century, better machines were built, which used the friction between a turning belt and one or two cylinders to generate charge. A modern version of these early friction machines is the **Van de Graaff generator**, which was invented in 1929 by the physicist Robert J. Van de Graaff at Princeton University in the United States. A version built in 1931 could produce an incredible million volts of charge. Modern versions can now be charged to five million volts!

THE SCIENCE YOU LEARN:
ELECTRICITY FROM STORM CLOUDS

During a thunderstorm, the storm clouds become highly charged in relation to the ground. Air is a good **insulator**, so it stops the charge on the clouds from leaking away. Eventually, the charge becomes so big that a giant spark jumps from the clouds to Earth (or from Earth to the clouds). This is lightning.

In 1752, the American scientist Benjamin Franklin did a famous experiment to show that electric charge built up in storm clouds. He hung a key from a kite string and flew it in a thunderstorm. Electricity from the storm clouds flowed into the key, down a wire attached to the kite string, and into a Leyden jar (see below). Franklin's experiment was incredibly dangerous. He could easily have been killed by a lightning strike on the kite. No modern scientist would ever attempt such an experiment and neither should you.

CASE STUDY

The Leyden jar

In 1745, a German priest called Ewald von Kleist found a way to store large amounts of electric charge. His device became known as a Leyden jar. It was a corked, glass jar, lined with metal. A metal rod through the cork was used to charge and discharge the jar. It was an early version of a **capacitor**, a device that is used to store charge in modern electrical equipment.

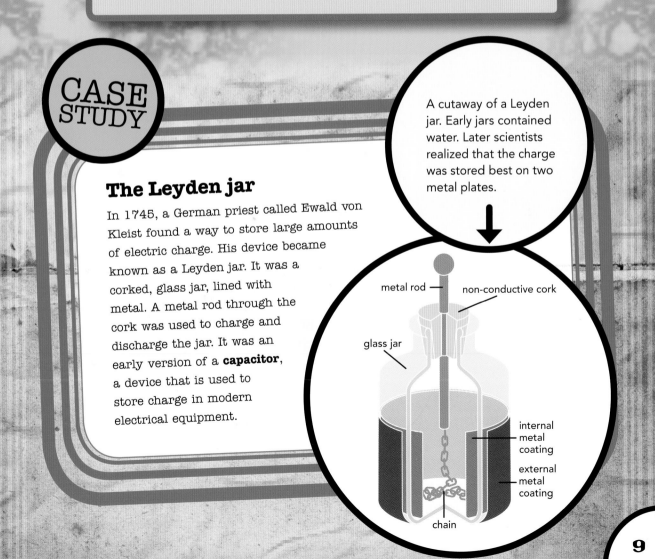

A cutaway of a Leyden jar. Early jars contained water. Later scientists realized that the charge was stored best on two metal plates.

metal rod — non-conductive cork

glass jar

internal metal coating

external metal coating

chain

Useful charges

Static electricity is used in many different ways in the modern world. Giving cars (and many other things) a thin, even coat of paint is one use. But how exactly does this involve static electricity? This spray painting is done using an electrostatic paint sprayer and works by charging the tiny droplets of paint as they leave the spray gun. The charged droplets are attracted to the metal surface of the unpainted car body, rather than left floating around in the air. When the droplets hit the car body, the charge in them quickly leaks away, because metal is a good **conductor**. The surface is left covered with a layer of uncharged, insulating paint, which does not attract charged paint droplets. So once an area of metal has been coated, no more paint is attracted to that area. The result is a thin, smooth coat that uses minimal amounts of paint.

Electrostatic charge is also essential to the working of photocopiers and laser printers. Both rely on a cylinder, or drum, which is given a positive electric charge. The parts of the drum that will be printed on are then given a negative charge. A very fine powder, called toner, is spread over the drum. The toner is positively charged, so it sticks to the negative parts of the drum, but is repelled from the areas of positive charge. Once the drum is "inked up" with toner, rollers press it against a piece of paper. The toner transfers onto the paper to create a copy of the pattern that was on the drum. Finally, heated rollers melt the toner onto the paper to make the printed or copied page permanent.

In a photocopier, the light and dark parts of a black and white image are turned into a pattern of electric charges on a drum.

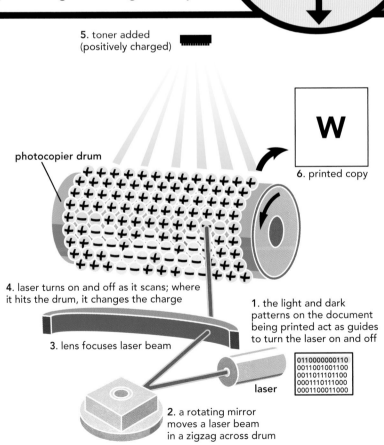

5. toner added (positively charged)

photocopier drum

6. printed copy

4. laser turns on and off as it scans; where it hits the drum, it changes the charge

3. lens focuses laser beam

1. the light and dark patterns on the document being printed act as guides to turn the laser on and off

laser

2. a rotating mirror moves a laser beam in a zigzag across drum

Cleaning the air

Static electricity is important in reducing industrial pollution from factories. Waste fumes often contain smoke and other tiny particles that can cause air pollution. An example is fly ash. When coal is burnt in a coal-fired power station, huge amounts of fly ash are produced. Power stations in the USA alone produce over 50 million tonnes of fly ash each year. Today, electrostatic precipitators (ESPs) remove 99.5 percent of fly ash from power station fumes. In an ESP, the waste fumes pass over a high-voltage wire that gives the particles in the fumes an electric charge. The fumes then pass between two plates – one positively charged and the other negatively charged. The charged particles are attracted to one of the plates and stick to it. This stops them from being released into the air.

This coal-fired power station uses ESPs to remove fly ash from its fumes. If the fly ash was not removed it would pollute the atmosphere.

Dangerous static

Static electricity is not always useful. For example, a static charge can damage electronic equipment, and static has to be avoided in places such as petrol stations, because it could cause a spark that could set light to the fuel.

One of the best ways of avoiding static is by grounding. Electric charge builds up on an object if it is electrically isolated and cannot get rid of its excess. Grounding means connecting an object to the ground with some kind of conductor, so that excess charge can flow away into the ground.

Battery power

A Leyden jar (see page 9) is like a battery. It can be charged using a friction machine, for example. Then, if you connect the metal foil on the outside of the jar with the metal rod on the top, there is a sudden flow of electricity.

The difference between a Leyden jar and a battery is that a Leyden jar has a certain amount of stored charge, which it discharges all in one go. A battery does not store charge. It produces electricity at a steady rate until it runs out, which can take many hours.

What is a battery?

A battery is a device that makes electricity through chemical reactions. Strictly, a battery is more than one electrical cell, but we often call single cells batteries, too. An electrical cell is made up of two **electrodes**, or poles – one negative, the other positive. These electrodes are usually made of two different metals. Between the two is a material called an electrolyte, which contains **ions** (charged atoms). When the battery is working, chemical reactions take place between the electrodes and the electrolyte. At one pole of the battery, the chemical reactions produce electrons, which travel out of the battery and around the electric circuit. At the other pole, the chemical reactions use up the electrons that stream into the battery.

A simple battery. The two electrodes are made of different metals separated by an electrolyte. The porous separator allows water to pass through, but not ions.

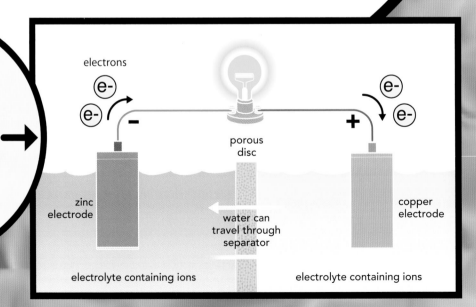

electrons

porous disc

zinc electrode

water can travel through separator

copper electrode

electrolyte containing ions

electrolyte containing ions

The first battery

In the late 18th century, the Italian scientist Luigi Galvani showed that a frog's leg hung on a copper hook would twitch when touched with a steel scalpel. Galvani thought that the twitching was caused by "animal electricity".

Another Italian scientist of the time, Alessandro Volta, disagreed. He thought that the animal tissue simply provided a special kind of connection between the two metals. After carrying out many experiments, Volta found that he could replace the frog's leg with a simple piece of cardboard soaked in brine (salty water). Using discs of copper and zinc, separated by brine-soaked cardboard, he built a device called a voltaic pile, which could produce a continuous flow of electricity. It was the first battery.

THE SCIENCE YOU LEARN: CURRENTS AND CIRCUITS

For an electrical device to work there has to be a circuit of electrical connections from the battery, to the device, and back to the battery.

A battery does not do much until two positive and negative poles (or terminals) are connected to form an electrical circuit. Then, a current flows through the wire. A circuit cannot be just a loop of wire. If it is, either the wire will overheat and break, or the battery will go flat very quickly. To work properly, there must be some kind of load or resistance in the circuit. The load is something like a light bulb or buzzer, which transforms the electrical energy from the battery into some other kind of energy, such as light or sound.

Electric elements

Alessandro Volta's invention of the battery (see page 13) was quickly picked up by other scientists who built their own versions of his voltaic pile. But what could it be used for? Besides, there were no electric lights, motors, or any other kind of electric device at the time. But batteries produce electricity through chemical reactions. If chemical reactions could be used to produce electricity, perhaps electricity could be used to drive chemical reactions? One person who investigated this idea was a British scientist called Humphry Davy.

Purifying aluminium

The process of using electricity to separate a chemical into simpler components is known as **electrolysis**. One of the most important uses of electrolysis today is to purify aluminium from its **ore**. Aluminium ore is known as **bauxite**. The bauxite is first partly purified, then dissolved in a molten aluminium compound called **cryolite**. Electricity is passed through this mixture. Molten aluminium purifies on the negative electrode, and is tapped off.

As well as building huge batteries and discovering new elements, Humphry Davy also made the first electric light, called an arc lamp (see page 41).

(see page 13)
(see page 41)

CASE STUDY

A compound discovery

Humphry Davy built a battery that was far more powerful than Volta's. He also found that if he passed an electric current through some substances they broke down into simpler substances. At first, he worked with substances dissolved in water. Then, he tried melting chemical compounds and passing electricity through them while they were molten. In 1807 and 1808, Davy made an amazing series of breakthroughs. He discovered the **elements** potassium and sodium, which until then had been unknown. He was also the first person to make pure forms of three other elements – barium, calcium, and strontium.

Until the electrolysis process was developed, aluminium was an extremely expensive metal because it was so hard to purify. The difficulty was that if bauxite was dissolved in water, electrolysis formed aluminium hydroxide instead of aluminium. Bauxite is mainly aluminium oxide, and this has a very high melting point, so doing the electrolysis on molten bauxite was not an option. Two young men, Charles Hall (helped by his sister Julia) in the USA, and Paul Héroult in France, both found the answer to the problem in 1886. By dissolving the bauxite in cryolite, they were able to carry out electrolysis at a relatively low temperature and produce pure aluminium.

The Oscars are the world's most famous film awards. Each Oscar is electroplated with copper (left), nickel (front), silver (right), and finally gold.

THE SCIENCE YOU LEARN: ELECTROPLATING

Electroplating involves laying a very thin layer of one metal on the surface of another metal. The object to be plated is made the negative electrode of an electric cell, while the metal to be used as a coating is part of the electrolyte. Electricity is passed through the cell, with the result that the metal that is in the electrolyte forms a thin layer on the surface of the **cathode**.

Electroplating has many uses. Chrome and nickel plating are used to give a bright finish to many steel objects. This also makes the steel more resistant to corrosion (rusting). Gold and silver plating are used in making jewellery. Gold and silver are very good electrical conductors and some electrical contacts are gold- or silver-plated to improve electrical connection.

Modern batteries

The batteries we use today are very different from those of Alessandro Volta or Humphry Davy. A modern battery can be smaller than a shirt button or bigger than a football pitch! Whatever the size, they all work on the basic idea of making electricity from chemical reactions.

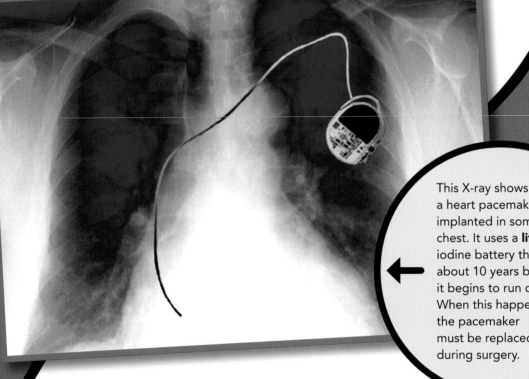

This X-ray shows a heart pacemaker implanted in someone's chest. It uses a **lithium** iodine battery that lasts about 10 years before it begins to run down. When this happens, the pacemaker must be replaced during surgery.

From lead to lithium

Different types of battery use different combinations of chemicals to produce batteries with different characteristics. Batteries can be divided into two basic types. Primary batteries are designed to be used just once. Secondary batteries are rechargeable. Look at the batteries you use at home. Which ones are primary and which are secondary?

Today's most common primary batteries are alkaline batteries. These rely on reactions between zinc and **manganese** dioxide to produce electricity. Alkaline batteries have a long life, and they work equally well for devices that need a lot of power and ones that use only a small amount of power. Other common kinds of primary battery include silver oxide and zinc–air batteries. Both of these batteries are small and are used in compact devices, such as watches and hearing aids.

The rechargeable equivalent of the alkaline battery is the nickel–cadmium battery. However, it has begun to be replaced by better rechargeable types, known as NiMH (nickel-metal **hydride**) and lithium ion batteries. Lithium ion batteries are light and very powerful for their size. They are the batteries used in laptops, mobile phones, and other kinds of digital equipment. A newer kind of lithium ion battery, known as a lithium ion polymer battery, has a plastic material in place of the electrolyte. The battery is lighter, it does not need a metal case, and it can be made in different shapes.

One of the oldest types of battery still in use is the lead-acid battery. This is the kind of battery that powers the electrics in vehicles. Lead-acid batteries were first made in 1859. They are quite large and heavy but are cheap to make, can be recharged many times, and can supply a large electric current.

Hybrid and electric cars have a different kind of battery from ordinary cars, because the battery has to power the car's electric motor as well as the normal car electrics. Hybrid cars usually have a lithium ion battery and a NiMH battery, while electric vehicles usually use a type of lithium battery.

An electric van being recharged. The lithium ion batteries in an electric vehicle delivers a high current to drive its powerful electric motor.

THE SCIENCE YOU LEARN:
VOLTAGE, CURRENT, AND RESISTANCE

Voltage is a measure of the electric potential a battery can provide. The higher a battery's voltage, the more electricity it can push through an electric circuit at a given resistance.

The current in a circuit is the amount of electrical charge passing through it every second. It is measured in amps (A). The current depends partly on the voltage of the battery, but also on the resistance in the circuit. If the current is 4 A and the resistance is doubled (and the voltage remains the same), the current will be halved to 2 A.

Fuel cells

Fuel cells are similar to batteries, but instead of containing all the chemicals needed within them, they are powered by a fuel – usually hydrogen or methane. The chemical reaction that makes a fuel cell work is between hydrogen in the fuel and oxygen from the air. The hydrogen and oxygen combine to form water. Water is the only waste product, so fuel cells do not pollute the air.

Many car manufacturers are developing road vehicles powered by fuel cells. This hybrid car is driven by a combination of a small petrol engine and an electric motor powered by a fuel cell.

CASE STUDY

Plastic batteries

In 1977, New Zealand chemist Alan MacDiarmid, U.S. physicist Alan Heeger, and Japanese chemist Hideki Shirakawa together developed a new type of plastic that conducts electricity. A similar type of plastic is used in the lithium ion polymer battery (see page 17). The latest type of plastic battery is being developed by Tayhas Palmore and Hyun-Kon Song, two engineers at Brown University, USA. The battery is about the size of a credit card, but thinner, and it can hold 100 times as much charge as an alkaline battery.

INVESTIGATION: MAKING A BATTERY

You can make a battery out of a lemon!

What you need:

- a lemon
- a copper coin
- a galvanized nail (one that is coated with zinc)
- a voltmeter (to show that it is working)

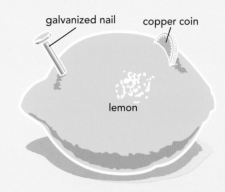

galvanized nail   copper coin

lemon

What to do:

1. Push the nail into one side of the lemon. Carefully cut a small slit in the other side and insert the coin. The nail and coin are the terminals.
2. Connect the free voltmeter across the terminals of your lemon battery. It should record a voltage of about 1 V. The coin is the positive pole of your battery, and the nail is the negative pole. If you connect the battery the wrong way round, the voltmeter will show a voltage of −1 V. One lemon makes a weak battery. By connecting six or seven lemon batteries together, with the nail on one lemon joined to the coin on the next, you can make a battery powerful enough to power a low-voltage LED (light-emitting diode).

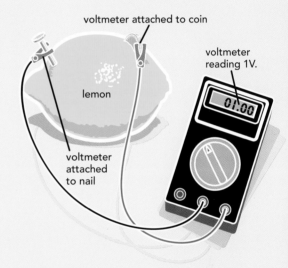

voltmeter attached to coin

voltmeter reading 1V.

lemon

voltmeter attached to nail

Lead batteries

In a lemon battery, the copper (positive) and zinc (negative) electrodes are connected through an acid electrolyte (lemon). A lead-acid car battery also has two metal electrodes connected via acid, but in this case the electrodes are lead (positive) and lead oxide (negative). A 12 V car battery is made up of six 2 V cells connected together. A car's battery can power most of its electrical functions, such as the headlights, tail lights, and stereo.

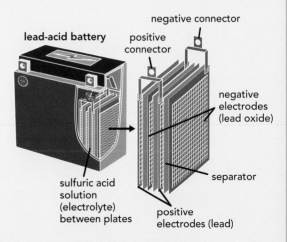

lead-acid battery   positive connector   negative connector

negative electrodes (lead oxide)

separator

sulfuric acid solution (electrolyte) between plates

positive electrodes (lead)

Magnets and wires

Batteries are useful sources of electricity. However, today nearly all the electricity we use is made in power stations by **generators**. Generators were developed about 30 years after the battery. They became possible in the 19th century, when scientists showed that electricity and magnetism were closely connected. The discovery and understanding of this connection is one of the most important discoveries in human history.

Michael Faraday (pictured right) thought that if an electric current in a wire produced a magnetic field, then perhaps a magnet could produce a current in a wire. He discovered that if a magnet was moved close to a wire, or a wire was moved through a magnetic field, an electric current was produced. This is the working principle behind modern electric generators. Faraday built a simple generator, which consisted of a copper disc that could rotate between the poles of a horseshoe magnet. Turning the disc produced an electric current.

THE SCIENCE YOU LEARN: ENERGY TRANSFERS

The Law of Conservation of Energy states that energy cannot be created or destroyed. In all devices that "produce" energy what is actually happening is that energy is being changed from one form into another. In Faraday's electric generator, the experimenter turns a handle that makes the copper disc go round. This, in turn, produces electricity. So the generator transforms the **kinetic** (movement) **energy** of the wheel into electrical energy.

Michael Faraday, the son of a blacksmith, became one of the most important of all English scientists.

Making the connection

Danish scientist, Hans Christian Orsted, was first to discover that electricity and magnetism were connected. In 1820, he was setting up an electrical demonstration for a lecture. He noticed that when a current was flowing through one of the wires, it moved the needle of a compass that was lying close to the wire. He suggested that the movement was caused by a magnetic field that formed around the wire whenever electricity was flowing.

Faraday was intrigued by Orsted's discovery and began his own investigations. He first showed that the magnetic field around an electric wire could be used to make the wire move. He fixed a permanent magnet in a dish of **mercury**, with an electric wire hanging into it (this kept the wire connected as part of a circuit). When electricity flowed through the wire, it produced a magnetic field around the wire. The magnetic field of the wire interacted with the field of the permanent magnet, making the wire move in a circle around the magnet. Faraday had built the first electric motor.

CUTTING EDGE: SAVING BRAKING ENERGY

Usually, when a car stops it does so using friction between a disc, or drum, on the wheel and a pair of brake pads. The kinetic energy of the car is lost as heat. This is why a car's brakes get hot. However, hybrid cars use a different system, known as regenerative braking. When you put your foot on the brake of a hybrid car, the car's electric power plant changes from a motor to a generator. The turning of the wheels is used to turn the generator and produce electricity. As we have already seen, generating electricity transforms kinetic energy into electricity. So instead of the car's movement being wasted as heat, regenerative braking uses it to charge the battery.

This Panasonic bicycle has a small electronic motor as well as pedals. It uses regenerative braking.

Magnets from electricity

A single electric wire produces only a weak magnetic field. However, if a wire is wound round and round many times to form a coil, it will produce a much stronger magnetic field when electricity travels through it. If the coil has an iron core through the centre it makes an even better magnet. The result is an electromagnet – a magnet that can be turned on and off at the flick of a switch. Electromagnets are used in modern electric generators, but they also have many other uses.

Being able to switch a magnet on and off is often a big advantage. For example, some types of scrapyard cranes use an electromagnet. The current can be switched on to pick up anything made of magnetic material (such as a car), and then switched off to drop it.

An **MRI** magnet is so powerful that it is unsafe to take anything made of iron or steel into the same room. Objects as big as oxygen tanks and stretchers have been pulled into the scanner magnet, and smaller metal objects can be pulled across the room at high speed!

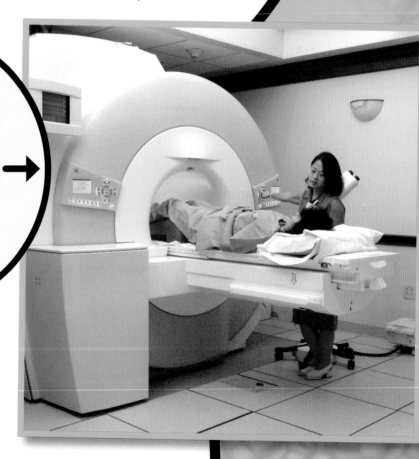

Supermagnets

The strongest kinds of electromagnets are superconducting magnets. At very low temperatures of about –243°C (–405°F), **superconductors** have no measurable resistance. In other words, a current flowing through a superconducting coil does not need a voltage to keep it flowing: it will keep going for years all by itself!

Almost the speed of light

The biggest electromagnets of all are used in the study of the fundamental particles of matter. Particle accelerators are used to study the particles that make up atoms, and to simulate conditions at the time of the **Big Bang**. They accelerate parts of atoms to close to the speed of light, then collide them with other particles travelling at high speed in the other direction. Most modern particle accelerators are circular and huge electromagnets are needed to bend the beams of particles as they travel around the accelerator.

The biggest of all particle accelerators is the Large Hadron Collider (LHC), which was completed in Switzerland in 2008. The magnets team had to build superconducting magnets bigger than any that had been made before. Italian scientist Lucio Rossi, who led the team, said: *"We introduced techniques including a welding method for stainless steel, and adapted state of the art technologies for large-scale production"*.

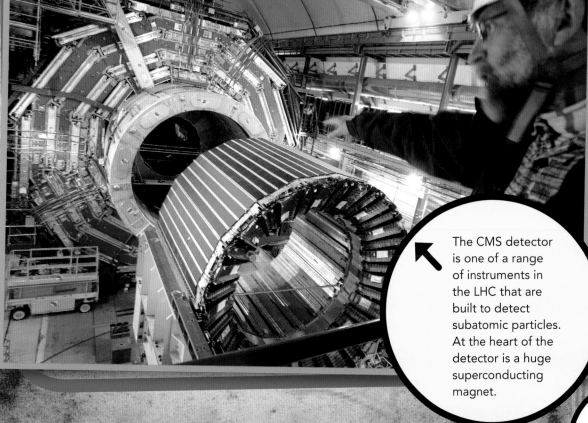

The CMS detector is one of a range of instruments in the LHC that are built to detect subatomic particles. At the heart of the detector is a huge superconducting magnet.

Modern generators

Generators and motors are two of the most important inventions of the last 200 years. Modern generators work on the same principles as Faraday's disc (see page 20). However, the design of modern generators and motors are very different from Faraday's originals.

Though there are many different generator types, all have two main parts: the **rotor**, and the **stator**. The rotor is free to turn and is surrounded by the stator. In large generators in power stations, the rotor is an electromagnet connected to its electricity supply through sliding contacts. The stator is a set of wire coils. A power source (see page 26) turns the rotor very quickly. Instead of wires moving and the magnet staying still, as in Faraday's disc, the magnet rotates while the wires remain still. The moving magnet creates a rapidly changing magnetic field, which produces an electric current in the wires of the stator.

In this very simple AC generator, the rotor is a single coil of wire, rotating between the poles of a large magnet. As the coil moves through the magnetic field, it **induces** an electric current.

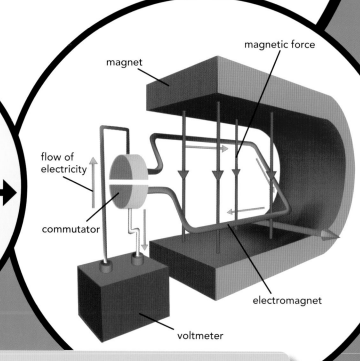

magnetic force

magnet

flow of electricity

commutator

electromagnet

voltmeter

 THE SCIENCE YOU LEARN: AC VERSUS DC

DC (direct current) electricity is like the current from a battery: it always flows in the same direction. However, modern generators produce AC (alternating current) – the current flows in one direction, then changes to flow in the opposite direction. In an AC the current changes direction rapidly – usually about 50 or 60 times a second. AC is much better than DC for distributing electricity through large networks (see page 37).

Electric motors

An electric motor is more or less a generator working in reverse. In the simplest kind of electric motor, a permanent magnet is the stator. It creates a magnetic field across a single coil of wire (the rotor). When a current flows through the coil, it creates a magnetic field around the wire that interacts with the field of the permanent magnet. This creates forces that push on the coil and make it rotate.

If the electric motor is powered by DC, it will only rotate until the magnetic fields of the coil and the permanent magnet line up: then it will stop. In order to keep going, a DC motor has to have special split contacts that reverse the current through the coil at least once every turn. This changes the magnetic field around the coil, and the magnetic forces once again push the coil around. In a motor driven by AC, the direction of the current is changing all the time, so it does not need split contacts.

In practical electric motors, as in generators, the magnetic field is created by an electromagnet rather than a permanent magnet, and the rotating coil has many turns.

In this simple electric motor, the coil on the left is part of an electromagnet that forms the stator, and the three coils on the right are part of the rotor.

CUTTING EDGE: SUPERCONDUCTING GENERATORS

Scientists in several countries are developing new kinds of generators that are made with superconducting materials. Researchers at the U.S. Air Force Research Laboratories have built a 1-megawatt superconducting generator that is lighter than a conventional generator, and is 97 percent efficient. Another group in Southampton, UK, has built a prototype generator that operates at −196°C (−321°F): a very high temperature for a superconducting device. This makes it much cheaper and simpler to keep cool.

Power from many sources

We now know how to generate electricity. But where does the power to turn the generator come from? The answer depends on the power station. Power stations range from small generators, driven by a wind **turbine**, to huge **hydroelectric** power plants. Different power stations use different energy sources to turn the generators. What they all have in common is that they are converting one type of energy into another.

Generating electricity in a thermal power station. Water is heated to steam in a boiler. The steam is used to turn turbines, which provide the power to turn the generator.

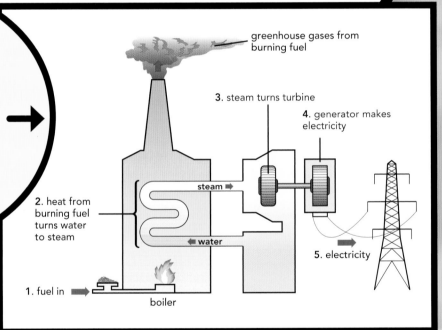

greenhouse gases from burning fuel

3. steam turns turbine

4. generator makes electricity

steam ➡

2. heat from burning fuel turns water to steam

◀ water

5. electricity

1. fuel in ➡

boiler

Thermal power

Most of the world's electricity is generated in thermal power stations. As the name suggests, thermal power stations turn heat into electricity. Some type of fuel is used to heat a boiler, where water is turned into steam. The steam turns a turbine, which turns the generator.

The majority of thermal power stations get their energy from oil, gas, or coal. These fuels have chemical energy locked up in the materials they are made from. When the fuels burn, the chemical energy is released, mainly as heat.

THE SCIENCE YOU LEARN: EFFICIENCY

The efficiency of a machine or process is a measure of how much useful work we get out of it, compared to how much energy is put in. The chain drive on a bike has a high efficiency of over 98 percent. Almost all energy someone uses to press down on the pedals of a bike goes into turning its wheels. Electric motors also have a high efficiency, sometimes up to about 90 percent.

In a steam turbine, or a car engine, or any kind of engine that uses heat to work, the efficiency can never be 100 percent. This is because the efficiency of any heat engine depends on the temperature of the working fluid (the steam or hot gases that make the engine work). A car engine, which works at a temperature of about 815°C (1,500°F) has a maximum efficiency of about 70 percent.

Nuclear power stations are also thermal power stations. The energy here is released by splitting the nuclei (centres) of the atoms of uranium fuel. The nuclear energy is released as heat, which is used to produce steam in a boiler.

In a few places, it is possible to get thermal power from the ground. In some areas, such as Iceland and parts of Italy and New Zealand, underground heat sources are close to Earth's surface. This heat can be used to make steam and power a generator.

Problems with fossil fuels

Fossil fuels are not an ideal energy source for making electricity. There are many problems with their use. Burning fossil fuels releases polluting gases into the atmosphere. It also produces carbon-dioxide (CO_2).This gas is found naturally in the atmosphere. However, humans are producing large amounts of extra CO_2 which has the effect of trapping the heat in the atmosphere. The increased level of CO_2 in the air is causing global climate change. Earth is gradually getting warmer, which is causing all kinds of problems worldwide. Climate change is one of the biggest challenges facing humanity in the 21st century.

Rising costs

Fossil fuels are also becoming increasingly expensive. Most of the oil, gas, and coal that is easy to extract has been used up. Most fossil fuels now have to be extracted from deep underground or below the seabed. There are still some reserves left in the ground, but supplies (particularly of oil) are gradually running out. Once fossil fuel supplies run out, they cannot be renewed or replaced. Fossil fuels took millions of years to form, and it would take a similar time for new supplies to develop.

Solar panels like these are called photovoltaic cells. They can be fitted to the roof of a building to generate electricity directly from sunlight.

Cleaner forms of energy

Fossil fuels are not the only energy source we can use to produce electricity. As we discover the problems caused by fossil fuels, people are turning to other ways of generating electricity. These "cleaner" forms of energy produce less carbon dioxide, and they use energy sources that are renewable or will not run out.

Hydroelectric power involves using the power of running water to produce electricity. A reservoir is formed by building a dam, and water from the reservoir is channelled along narrow tunnels to water turbines. The high-pressure water spins the turbines, which in turn spins the rotors of the generators.

Hydroelectricity has been the most successful form of "clean" electricity generation. Power from rivers and streams is unlikely to run out, and hydroelectric power generation does not produce carbon dioxide. However, there is a limit to how much more hydroelectric power we can produce. On some large rivers, there are already so many hydroelectric dams that hardly any water actually reaches the sea!

Wind power and solar power are two "clean" energy sources that are developing quickly. Wind turbines (see page 32) transform the power of the wind (kinetic energy) into electricity. Solar power stations can be one of two kinds: some use photovoltaic (PV) cells to turn the Sun's energy directly into electricity; while solar thermal power stations focus sunlight to heat water and produce steam.

Two other ways of getting power from water are by tidal and wave energy. These may become important sources of energy for power generation in the future. However, at present they are not well developed, and produce only very small amounts of electricity worldwide.

CUTTING EDGE: CARBON CAPTURE AND STORAGE (CCS)

One way of reducing the damaging impact of fossil fuel power stations on the environment would be to "capture" carbon dioxide before it is released into the air, and then safely store it somewhere. Capturing carbon dioxide can be done either by "scrubbers" that remove it from exhaust gases, or by changing the fuel before it is burnt, so that the carbon dioxide can be captured more easily. The carbon dioxide can then be stored either in the ground or deep in the ocean.

All the different stages of CCS are feasible, but at present no power stations are using the whole system. A report by the Intergovernmental Panel on Climate Change (IPCC) says that CCS could contribute between 15 and 55 percent of the total carbon dioxide reductions we need to make by 2100.

More efficient generation

Generating electricity in thermal power stations is not very efficient. Two ways of improving the efficiency of thermal power are to use combined-cycle power stations, or CHP (combined heat and power) generation.

In combined-cycle power stations, gas or another fuel is burned to heat air. The air then powers a gas turbine. Gas turbines run at high temperatures, so the exhaust gases from the gas turbine are still very hot. They can be used to heat water in a boiler and power a steam turbine. The combination of a high-temperature gas turbine with a low-temperature steam turbine is more efficient than using a steam turbine alone. Combined-cycle power stations can reach efficiencies of around 65 percent.

In a combined-cycle power station fuel is used to heat gases for a gas turbine. The exhaust gases from this turbine are very hot and can be used to make steam to drive a steam turbine.

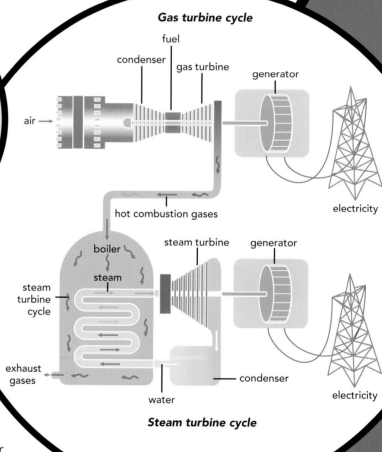

The steam that comes out of a steam turbine is still quite hot. In a conventional power station, it has to be cooled in giant cooling towers before it can be used again. The steam cannot be used to make more electricity. However, it can be used in other ways. In CHP generation, the heat remaining after power generation is used to heat nearby homes and offices. If combined-cycle generation and CHP are used together, efficiency rises to over 90 percent.

Spinning blades

In most kinds of power station, the device that actually spins the generator is a turbine. A turbine is a kind of fan. It has two, three, or sometimes hundreds of blades. Different kinds of turbine work best with different kinds of energy source.

Steam turbines are used in thermal power stations. A steam turbine is made up of many individual rotors that work together. Each individual rotor has hundreds of small blades. Some of the rotors are fixed and others can spin. The fixed blades direct the steam going through the steam turbine so that it hits the rotors that can spin at the best angle.

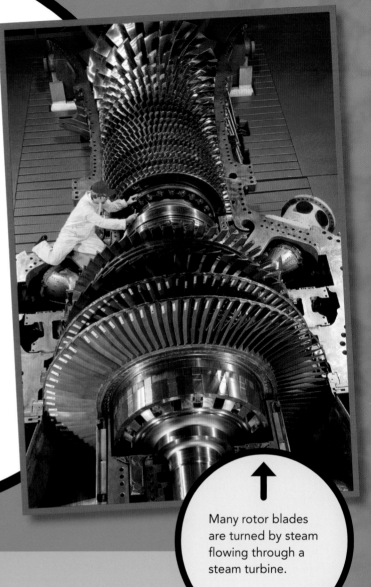

Many rotor blades are turned by steam flowing through a steam turbine.

SCIENCE AROUND US:
VERSATILE TURBINES

Turbines are not just used in power stations. They have many other uses.

- Many cars have a turbocharger. This is a turbine driven by the car's exhaust gas, which compresses the air going into the engine. This makes the engine produce more power.
- Dentists use very small drills for drilling and polishing teeth. These tiny drills are driven by compressed air. The air spins a small turbine, which turns the drill.
- Even vacuum cleaners use turbines! Some types of vacuum cleaner have a "turbo" head. Some of the air sucked in through the head is used to turn a small air turbine. The turbine turns a rotating brush.

See how many things you can find at home or at school that use turbines.

Other types of turbine

Gas turbines are similar to steam turbines, but the rotors are smaller and lighter. As in a steam turbine there are fixed and rotating parts.

Wind turbines usually have two or three large blades, which turn quite slowly. Inside the generator, a gearbox converts the slow turning of the turbine blades into rapid spinning for the generator. Generally, the faster a generator can spin, the more electricity it will produce.

The water turbines used in hydroelectricity plants often have more blades, but there are several different designs. Different types of water turbine work best with different heads of water (the head is the vertical height of water available to power the turbine).

New ideas

Scientists around the world are working on the challenge of finding ways to replace fossil fuels for electricity generation. One promising new idea is to generate electricity from waste water using microbial fuel cells (MFCs). Researchers at Pennsylvania State University, USA, have developed a practical MFC that produces small amounts of electricity.

A fuel cell is a device similar to a battery that produces electricity from hydrogen or some other fuel. In an MFC, the fuel is replaced by bacteria and organic waste. The bacteria "eat" the waste, and in the process produce electricity. The MFC cleans the waste water at the same time as producing electricity.

This large wind farm has hundreds of wind turbines. Each turbine catches the wind and turns a generator.

Another new idea being developed at Swansea University in Wales, UK, is paint that can generate electricity from sunlight. It works when painted on steel surfaces. This "solar paint" is promising because it produces electricity at quite low light levels. This would make it useful in climates where it is often cloudy or rainy.

Researchers are investigating many other new ways of producing electricity, including clothing that generates electricity, electricity from rainfall, and electrodynamic tethers (see the case study below). Some of these ideas will be impractical, but others may become important methods of electricity generation in the future.

CASE STUDY

Space tether

In theory, we should be able to make use of Earth's magnetic field to generate electricity. This is the idea behind the electrodynamic tether. The tether is basically a very long wire, hanging from a spacecraft, orbiting Earth. As the spacecraft orbits, the wire moves through Earth's magnetic field, so electricity is generated. If the process is reversed, the tether can be used to propel the spacecraft. Electricity is passed through the tether, and this produces a force that moves the spacecraft.

Tether experiments were carried out on space shuttle missions in 1992 and 1996. On the second mission the tether broke and the experiment failed, but useful lessons were learned.

This was the first space shuttle flight to try out a space tether in 1992. The tether worked, but it was much shorter than the one tried in 1996.

Electricity where it is needed

We often take the electricity supply to our homes for granted. But the networks that distribute electricity are an incredible engineering triumph. Electricity distribution is about getting electricity to where it is needed. Millions of homes and businesses expect to have electricity available at all times, even if a power line is cut or an electricity substation breaks down. People also expect to be able to use as much electricity as they need, whenever they need it. Keeping all these customers happy is a tricky job that involves a lot of planning and a very flexible electricity network.

Electricity grid

The network of lines that carries electricity from power stations to homes, offices, and factories is called an electricity grid. The grid includes many large power stations and also many smaller generators. Cables carry electricity from each power station to thousands or millions of customers. The customers and power stations are connected in a complex network.

Controlling the electricity grid involves many engineers and a large computer system. The amount of electricity the grid uses varies all the time, depending on the time of day, the time of year, the weather, and what is happening in the world.

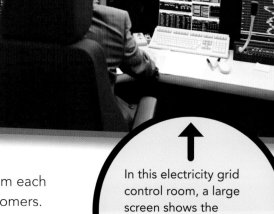

In this electricity grid control room, a large screen shows the main electricity lines throughout the country.

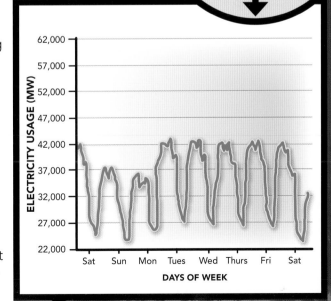

Distributed generation

Electricity grids mainly involve large power stations providing electricity for thousands of homes and businesses. However, there are an increasing number of distributed energy producers. These are producers making electricity for a small area or even for a single building, using methods such as solar and wind power, CHP (see page 30), or small-scale hydroelectricity.

Advocate South Suburban Hospital in Hazel Crest, Illinois, USA, is an example of how distributed generation can work. The hospital has two CHP generating systems using gas turbines. Together they can provide all the power the hospital needs at peak times. The CHP generators work only on weekdays during the day. At night and at the weekend, the generators shut down and the hospital uses mains electricity. The distributed system saves the hospital more than $200,000 (£112,400) in bills each year, and means that it has secure electricity generation if there are power cuts.

A graph showing electricity use over a week for the whole UK. Each night electricity use drops, then rises during the day.

Engineers have to carefully watch how electricity use is changing, and make sure they have enough electricity being generated to keep everyone supplied. It is difficult to store large amounts of electricity. If there is high demand for electricity, it has to be generated at the time.

A group of large power stations, producing a fairly constant level of power, supply most of the electricity we use. Sudden peaks and troughs in demand are met by power stations that can quickly start up and shut down, for example, ones that use gas turbines.

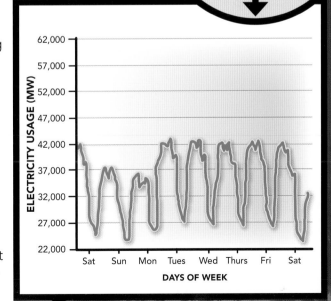

Pumped storage

Another way that electricity can be supplied quickly when demand suddenly grows is by using pumped storage. Pumped storage is a kind of hydroelectric power. The power station has two reservoirs, one high up and one lower down. Water from the higher reservoir flows through pipes to the lower reservoir, and water turbines generate electricity. But the turbines can also act as pumps, pushing the water back to the higher reservoir. When electricity demand is low, spare power can be used to pump water from the lower reservoir to the upper one. Then when the grid needs more electricity, the process can be reversed to generate electricity.

Dinorwig pumped storage station was built in the mountains of north Wales, UK. In order to avoid damaging the environment, the generator hall was built underground.

CASE STUDY

The battle of the currents

In the United States during the 1880s, Edison's DC power stations were challenged by a system using AC power. Inventor and businessman George Westinghouse developed this new system with an AC electric motor and AC transformers, both invented by Nikola Tesla.

AC power systems soon gained favour as they could transmit electricity further and used less power. Edison tried to show that AC electricity was more dangerous by publicly electrocuting stray cats and dogs. His campaign failed. In 1895, Westinghouse successfully built a huge hydroelectric power station at Niagara Falls that supplied electricity for the whole city of Buffalo. This was the end for Edison's DC generators.

Long-distance cables

Edison's Pearl Street power station in New York (see page 5) had six powerful jumbo dynamos pumping out electricity. But it could not supply customers more than about 3 km (2 miles) from the power station, because the dynamos produced DC electricity at a fairly low voltage of about 100 V. Over long distances, most of the electricity was lost in transmission.

Modern generators produce AC electricity. The advantage of AC is that the voltage of the electricity can be changed easily, using a **transformer** (see page 38). At very high voltages, electricity can be transmitted long distances with minimal losses. So electricity leaving the power station is "stepped up" to voltages over 110,000 V before being transmitted. For transmission over very long distances, the voltage may be as high as 1,100,000 V. Cables are often carried above ground on tall pylons, but in some places are buried underground or laid underwater.

Once the electricity is close to where it is needed, a series of transformers step the voltage down to lower values. Different customers need electricity at different voltages. Heavy industry and railways use electricity at 11,000 V, while light industry uses a 600 V supply. The electricity we get in our homes is at an even lower voltage. European, Asian, and African countries use a voltage of around 230 V, whereas in Japan, North America, and some parts of South America the voltage is between 100 and 127 V.

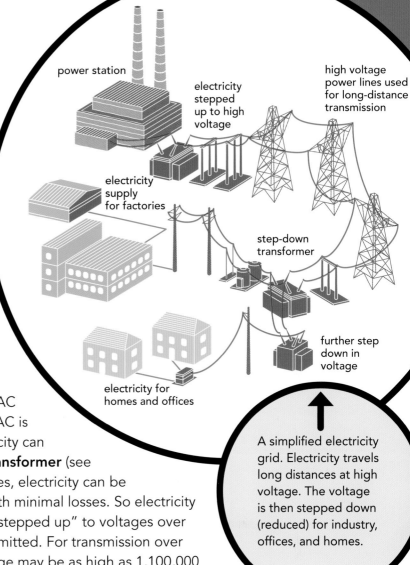

power station

electricity stepped up to high voltage

high voltage power lines used for long-distance transmission

electricity supply for factories

step-down transformer

further step down in voltage

electricity for homes and offices

A simplified electricity grid. Electricity travels long distances at high voltage. The voltage is then stepped down (reduced) for industry, offices, and homes.

Two coils of wire

Transformers are a vital part of any electricity distribution system. So how do they work? In its most basic, two coils of wire placed closely together create a transformer. It works by a process known as **induction**. Passing AC electricity through the first coil induces a current in the second coil.

The size of the two coils in the transformer affects the voltage going in and out of it. If the voltage going into the transformer is 110 V, and the second coil of the transformer has twice as many turns as the first coil, then the voltage coming out of the transformer will be doubled to 220 V. However, if the second coil has only half as many turns as the first coil, the voltage coming out of the transformer will be half of 110 V, or 55 V.

The voltage is not the only thing that changes from one side of the transformer – the current changes, too. When the voltage doubles in a step-up transformer, the current is halved. Similarly, when the voltage goes down, the amount of current flowing goes up. This explains why transforming electricity to a high voltage makes it easier to send it long distances. If the voltage is stepped up say, ten times, the current will be reduced to a tenth of its original value. A small current can be transmitted in a cable much smaller than that needed to transmit a large current, and with less power loss in transmission.

Inside the plug of a mobile phone charger is a transformer that changes the voltage of the mains electricity to match that of the phone.

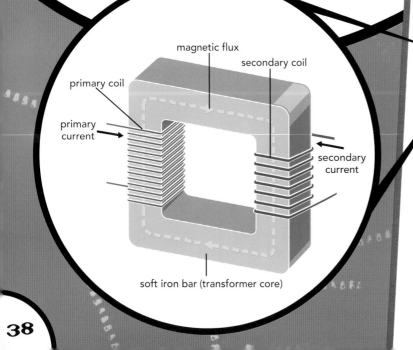

magnetic flux

secondary coil

primary coil

primary current

secondary current

soft iron bar (transformer core)

Going back to DC

When electricity is sent long distance through AC cables, the power losses begin to get quite large, even at high voltages. One solution to this problem is to go back to DC transmission. In Edison's time it was not possible to change the voltage of DC electricity. However this can now be done using voltage converters. High-voltage DC (HVDC) electricity can be transmitted over long distances with much smaller losses than with AC. Today, HVDC connections are used to transmit electricity to or from isolated places, or to connect together two electricity grids that are not directly compatible. An important use of HVDC in the future could be for offshore wind farms. Several countries have plans to build large groups of wind generators at sea. HVDC is probably the best way of getting electricity from the wind generators to shore.

CUTTING EDGE: SHORE-TO-PLATFORM POWER

Many oil and gas production platforms work far out at sea. They often produce their own electricity using gas turbines. However, the turbines are large and noisy, and produce large amounts of polluting carbon dioxide. The Troll-A gas production platform is 70 km (43.4 miles) from the coast of Norway. In 2005, it became the first offshore platform to get electricity from the mainland via an HVDC link. Asmund Maeland of the power company ABB was involved in developing the HVDC link. Maeland says that it is much smaller and lighter than a normal HVDC system, and there is no physical limit on how far the electricity can be transmitted.

The Troll-A oil drilling platform gets electricity from the shore via a special lightweight HVDC electricity line. It is the first line of its kind in the world.

Electricity users

We use electricity everywhere: in homes, offices, factories, on the streets, and in cars and other vehicles. Every year, the world produces over 17 million billion watt hours of electricity. This is enough energy to run about 13 billion personal computers continuously for a whole year! What do we do with all this electricity?

Factories of all kinds use large amounts of electricity. The knitting machines used in this textiles factory are powered by electric motors. ➡

Changing energy

Energy from any electrical device can be transformed in some way. Electric motors, for instance, convert electricity into movement. We use large motors to power trains and machines in factories, and smaller motors in vacuum cleaners, washing machines, and many other things in the home.

Another common way of transforming electric energy is to turn it into heat. Cookers and microwaves, room heaters, and water heaters are common devices that turn electricity to heat. Electric heaters contain wires that have a high resistance (electricity does not pass through them easily). The effort involved in forcing electricity through the wire heats it up.

Electricity can also be changed to light and sound. Loudspeakers use electromagnets (see page 22) to convert electricity into sound, and there are many different ways of changing electricity to light (see page 41). Lighting, music systems, televisions, mobile phones, and many other devices transform electricity into light, sound, or both.

Modern arc lamps are small, efficient, and produce a very bright light. They are used in the headlights of many luxury cars.

Arc lamps

The earliest power stations were set up to provide electric light, and lighting is still an important use of electricity. The first electric lights were called arc lamps. They were developed by Humphry Davy in the early 19th century. Early arc lamps produced a very harsh light and used large amounts of electricity, so had limited use. The real breakthrough came in 1878–79, when Thomas Edison, in the USA, and Joseph Swan, in the UK, both developed filament bulbs (or incandescent lights) – better known as conventional light bulbs.

CUTTING EDGE: WIRELESS ELECTRICITY

Professor Marin Soljacic and other researchers at MIT (Massachusetts Institute of Technology) in the USA have discovered a way to send electricity from place to place without wires. The electricity is transmitted using radio waves. Soljacic said: *"There are so many autonomous devices, such as mobile phones and laptops, that have emerged in the last few years. We started thinking, it would be really convenient if you didn't have to recharge these things"*.

Filament bulbs

Incandescent lights are conventional light bulbs. They were an important form of lighting in the 20th century and are still widely used today. However, incandescent light bulbs produce a lot of heat, as well as producing light. This makes them inefficient, because the electrical energy that is turned into heat is not doing useful work. Many people are now replacing incandescent lights with low-energy bulbs.

Neon lighting in O'Hare Airport in Chicago, USA. Neon lights are similar to fluorescent lights, but the colour comes from the gas inside the tube rather than a coating on the tube.

Fluorescent lights

Low-energy light bulbs are compact fluorescent lights. They are similar to the fluorescent tubes that have been used for many years in offices and other larger buildings. A fluorescent tube contains a mixture of a gas at low pressure and mercury vapour (mercury is a liquid at normal temperatures, but it turns into a vapour or gas at low pressure). When the light is turned on, electricity makes the gas and mercury vapour produce ultra-violet radiation. This hits the fluorescent coating covering the inside of the tube, and stimulates it to produce light.

Low-energy bulbs are almost six times as efficient as incandescent lights. A 12 W low-energy bulb is as bright as a 60 W incandescent bulb. They also last far longer, up to 30,000 hours of use, compared to 1,000 to 2,000 hours for an incandescent bulb. For these reasons, low-energy bulbs have begun to replace incandescent bulbs for household lighting. However, a third kind of lighting, the light-emitting diode (LED), may soon replace low-energy fluorescent bulbs.

CUTTING EDGE : PLASTIC LEDS

OLEDs (organic LEDs) are made from plastic instead of semiconductors. They can be made into a thin sheet, which makes them ideal for screens and visual displays. OLEDs are already being used in some mobile phones and MP3 players. The first OLED television went on sale in 2007.

LEDs

An LED is a **semiconductor device**, like the transistors, diodes, and other components used in electronics. When electricity passes through the LED, it lights up. LEDs have been used as lights for many years.

Modern LED lights are used for torches, bicycle lights, large screen displays, emergency lights on police cars and ambulances, and in many other ways. LEDs are more expensive than low-energy lights, and not quite as efficient. However, they last longer and are less easily damaged.

This TV has a screen made from OLEDs. OLED screens are brighter and give a sharper image than other kinds of flat screens.

Electricity at home

Electricity has a long and complicated journey, from the power station where it is generated, to your house. When it comes into your house, the electricity supply cable connects to something known as a consumer unit. This is a device that divides the supply between several different circuits, all separated from one another.

The lights in your house use relatively little power, so they do not need a large current to make them work. In some countries, the lights are on separate circuits with thinner wires that allow only a few amps to flow through them.

Electrical sockets need more power than the lights. Lights rarely use more than 100 W, but a computer uses about 500 W, and a vacuum cleaner may use 2,000 W. In some countries the sockets are connected in a circle, known as a ring main. This method means that each socket has two sets of wires connecting it to the mains. With double wiring, each individual wire is less likely to become overloaded. Circuits can be protected by circuit breakers, which stop electricity flow if too much current starts to flow through the wires. Devices, such as electric cookers, water heaters, and showers use even more power than the mains sockets. Each of these has its own circuit.

In some U.S. homes indoor lights are on the same circuits as the power sockets and do not have their own dedicated circuit.

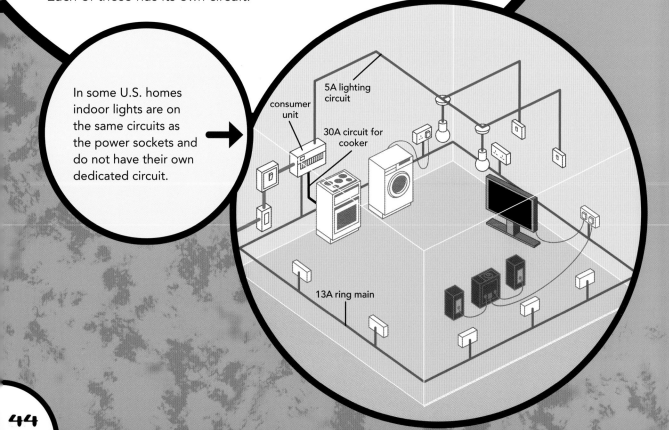

consumer unit

5A lighting circuit

30A circuit for cooker

13A ring main

If too many things are turned on at once, or if something goes wrong with an electrical device, it may cause a large current to flow through the wires. If the current is too large the wires get hot. This could damage the wiring and cause a fire.

The wiring in a house is designed to protect against this kind of accident. Each of the circuits in a consumer unit is protected by a special switch known as a circuit-breaker. The circuit-breaker allows a specific maximum current level for that particular circuit. For example, a lighting circuit might allow a maximum current of 5 A. If something goes wrong, and too much current flows in the circuit, the circuit-breaker switch trips, and cuts the current altogether.

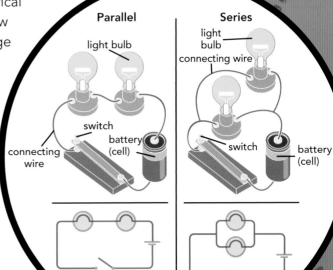

The components of two bulbs connected in parallel and in series are shown in the top drawings. The circuit diagrams are below.

THE SCIENCE YOU LEARN:
SERIES AND PARALLEL CIRCUITS

When there is more than one component in an electric circuit, there are two ways of connecting them together. They can be connected in series, or in parallel. In a series circuit, the different components are connected one after the other. In a parallel circuit they are connected side by side.

As more devices are connected into a series circuit, the voltage (amount of energy) available to each device drops. If two light bulbs are connected in series to a battery, they shine more dimly than a single bulb.

In a parallel circuit, each component gets the same voltage, so two light bulbs connected in parallel shine as brightly as one. However, the circuit takes more current, so a battery powering two lightbulbs in parallel runs down more quickly than with one bulb.

The electrical sockets and lights in a building are connected together in parallel. If they were connected in series, all the lights would dim every time another light was turned on.

Summary

In little more than 100 years, electricity has become our most important and useful way of transmitting and supplying energy. We have seen how all this only became possible because of key scientific discoveries made in the early 19th century (see page 21). These discoveries showed how electricity and magnetism are connected. Generators, electric motors, transformers, and many of the other essential parts of the electricity system are based on the electromagnetic connection.

Electricity is such a useful and flexible source of energy because it can be transformed in so many ways – into sound, light, heat, movement, or into radio waves, X-rays, or other kinds of electromagnetic radiation. All the electrical devices we use involve transforming electrical energy in this way. Electricity can also be used in chemical processes, such as electrolysis and electroplating (see page 15).

The energy we use to make electricity comes from a variety of sources, but the main one is fossil fuels (see page 28). The pollution from fossil fuels, and the climate change that this is causing, are creating huge problems for humans worldwide. Part of the solution to these problems lies in producing electricity using "clean" forms of energy that do not produce pollution. Improving the efficiency of how we generate and use electricity could also help, by reducing the amount of electricity we need.

An electric future

Research into electricity promises some exciting developments in the future. We may soon be able to get rid of plugs and wires and power everything using wireless electricity. OLED screens (see page 43) may soon be flexible enough to roll up and carry around. Electric clothes could soon be powering mobile phones, MP3 players, and other personal electric devices.

The water from this well is pumped up using solar power. It gives people clean drinking water without causing pollution.

The way that we generate electricity is likely to change rapidly in the near future. If we are going to reduce our use of fossil fuels, we need many new generators to produce electricity. It is likely that in future there will be many more smaller producers feeding electricity into the grid. Some will use clean, renewable energy sources, such as wind, solar, or water power, to produce electricity. Other producers will generate electricity from waste, using microbial fuel cells (see page 32). We need to make the right choices and use electricity to help solve the energy crisis, not to make it worse.

An important part of changing the way we generate and use electricity is to change our attitudes. We live in a world where the richest, most successful nations, with the most resources and the best research facilities, are using far more electricity than the poorest countries. If we can change our point of view, so that using less energy is a sign of success, we have a good chance of solving the challenges of the future.

Facts and figures

Timeline of electricity development

Date	Event
600 BC	Greek mathematician Thales of Miletus discovers that a piece of amber, when rubbed with a cloth, attracts small objects. This is the first known description of static electricity.
1600	English doctor and scientist William Gilbert coins the term electricity.
c. 1660	German scientist and inventor Otto von Guericke invents a simple machine for producing static electricity. The machine rubs a pad against a large ball of sulfur to create an electric charge.
1745–46	Pieter van Musschenbroek of the Netherlands develops the Leyden jar. It is named after Leyden University, where he worked.
1752	U.S. scientist and politician Benjamin Franklin carries out his famous kite experiment, showing that lightning is a form of electricity. Franklin is also the first to talk about positive and negative electric charges.
1800	Italian physicist Alessandro Volta builds his voltaic pile, the first practical battery.
1805	Italian chemist Luigi Brugnatelli invents electroplating. He uses a voltaic pile to plate two silver medals with gold.
c. 1808	English scientist Humphry Davy invents the first electric light – the carbon arc lamp.
1820	Danish physicist and chemist Hans Christian Orsted discovers that moving a wire in a magnetic field induces an electric current in the wire. French scientists André-Marie Ampère and François Arago independently make the same discovery.
1826	While still a schoolteacher, German physicist Georg Ohm discovers how electrical voltage, current, and resistance are related to each other.

Date	Event
1828	First practical electric motor is built by Hungarian engineer and inventor Ányos Jedlik.
1831	Michael Faraday demonstrates the principles of the electric generator and electric motor.
1832	French instrument-maker Hippolyte Pixii makes a practical generator, which produces electricity when a crank is turned by hand.
1835	U.S. scientist Joseph Henry invents the electrical relay, which boosts an electrical signal sent along a wire. This makes it possible to send electrical signals long distances and is the basis of the electric telegraph.
1860s	Scottish mathematician James Clerk Maxwell develops a mathematical explanation of the relationship between electricity and magnetism, and shows that light is a kind of electromagnetic wave. His work underpins the later development of electric power, radios, and television.
1878–1880	English scientist Joseph Swan and U.S. inventor Thomas Edison both develop incandescent light bulbs with a carbon filament.
1882	Thomas Edison opens the Pearl Street power station in New York City, USA, one of the world's first central electric power plants. Pearl Street produces DC electricity. It can power 5,000 lights, but they have to be close to the power station.
1883	First electric railway is built in Brighton, UK, by Magnus Volk.
1893	Croatian-born U.S. inventor Nikola Tesla demonstrates the first AC electrical system, including a generator, transformers, transmission system, motor, and lights.
1895–96	Niagara Falls hydroelectric power station opens in the United States. Using AC power generation, it can send electricity to customers over 32.2 km (20 miles) away in Buffalo, New York.
1898	U.S. inventor Daniel McFarlan Moore (1869–1933) demonstrates the first fluorescent lamps, which use carbon dioxide to produce a white light, or nitrogen to produce a pink light.

Date	Event
1899	Waldmar Jungner invents the rechargeable nickel-cadmium battery.
1901	Thomas Edison invents the alkaline storage battery.
1908	James Murray Spangler, a U.S. inventor who works as a caretaker, invents the first portable electric vacuum cleaner.
1909	World's first pumped storage power station opens in Switzerland.
1911	Superconductivity discovered by Dutch physicist Heike Kamerlingh Onnes.
1933	German researchers Walter Meissner and Robert Ochsenfeld discover that a superconducting material will repel a magnetic field. This later leads to the use of superconductors in maglev (magnetic levitation) trains.
1934	Coiled-coil electric light bulb invented; this increases the amount of radiated light.
1934	U.S. engineer George Inman leads a team at the General Electric Company that develop the modern fluorescent light.
1954	First solar cell invented by Daryl Chapin, Calvin Fuller, and Gerald Pearson of Bell Laboratories.
1962	U.S. electrical engineer Nick Holonyak invents the light-emitting diode (LED).
1977	Japanese physicist Hideki Shirakawa, and Americans Alan MacDiarmid and Alan Heeger, discover organic polymers that conduct electricity. This leads to the production of plastic batteries, LEDs, and solar cells.
2008	The world's largest particle accelerator, the Large Hadron Collider, begins operation.

Electricity consumption: top 20 countries

Rank	Country	Electricity used (billion kWh)*
1	USA	3,816
2	China	2,859
3	Russia	985
4	Japan	974
5	Germany	545
6	Canada	540
7	India	488
8	France	451
9	South Korea	369
10	Brazil	368
11	UK	349
12	Italy	307
13	Spain	243
14	South Africa	241
15	Taiwan	221
16	Australia	220
17	Mexico	183
18	Ukraine	182
19	Saudi Arabia	147
20	Iran	136

Source: CIA Factbook, based on information from 2005–2007
* kWh = kilowatt hours. 1 kilowatt hour = 3,600,000 joules.

Top 20 hydroelectricity producers

Rank	Country	Hydroelectricity production (billion kWH)	Rank	Country	Hydroelectricity production (billion kWH)
1	China	396.99	11	France	51.18
2	Canada	359.88	12	Paraguay	50.65
3	Brazil	334.08	13	Colombia	39.41
4	USA	270.32	14	Turkey	39.17
5	Russia	172.86	15	Austria	35.52
6	Norway	134.44	16	Argentina	33.92
7	India	99.00	17	Italy	33.27
8	Japan	77.43	18	Switzerland	30.91
9	Venezuela	74.28	19	Pakistan	30.55
10	Sweden	72.08	20	Mexico	27.46

Source: Energy Information Administration (EIA), latest data 2005

Top 15 producers of renewable energy (geothermal, solar, wind, wood, and waste electric power)

Rank	Country	Renewable energy production (billion kWH)	Rank	Country	Renewable energy production (billion kWH)
1	USA	99.68	8	Denmark	10.07
2	Germany	42.85	9	Canada	10.05
3	Japan	23.30	10	Mexico	9.45
4	Spain	23.17	11	Philippines	9.41
5	Brazil	18.33	12	Finland	9.35
6	UK	15.02	13	Sweden	8.83
7	Italy	14.22	14	Netherlands	8.64
			15	India	7.68

Source: Energy Information Administration (EIA), latest data 2005

Find out more

Books

Awesome Experiments in Electricity and Magnetism, Michael DiSpezio (Sterling Juvenile, 2006)

Electricity and Magnetism, Andrew Solway (Wayland, 2007)

Fully Charged: Electricity (Everyday Science), Steve Parker (Heinemann Library, 2004)

Fusion: Blackout!, Anna Claybourne (Heinemann Library, 2005)

Shocking Electricity (Horrible Science), Nick Arnold (Scholastic Hippo, 2000)

Thomas Edison: Inventor of the Age of Electricity, Linda Tagliaferro (Lerner Publications, 2003)

Websites

- *www.bbc.co.uk/schools/ks2bitesize/science/activities/changing_circuits*
  BBC school science clips, with animations in which you can alter series or parallel circuits and see the effect this has.

- *thefusebox.ce-electricuk.com/page/electricity/index.cfm*
  A website with interactive animations to help you understand about electricity.

- *www.wvic.com/how-gen-works.htm*
  Check out this interactive animation to show how an electronic generator works.

Topics for further study

The U.S. scientist and politician Benjamin Franklin did an experiment to show that lightning was electricity. What did he do to prove the connection between electricity and lightning?

Motors and generators are not the only electromagnetic devices that we use. Find out how electric bells, microphones, and loudspeakers rely on a combination of electricity and magnetism.

The Dinorwig pumped storage station is an amazing feat of engineering. See if you can find out more about it. What about other hydroelectric power stations? What are the stories behind the building of the Hoover Dam in the United States and the Itaipu Dam in South America?

Glossary

amber   yellow-gold clear substance formed from the hardened sap of certain trees

atom   one of the fundamental particles from which everything is made

bauxite   rock rich in aluminium

Big Bang   way in which some scientists think the Universe began

capacitor   component of many electronic circuits. Capacitors can store electric charge.

cathode   negatively charged electrode which electrons use to enter an electrical device

conductor   material that allows electricity to flow through it easily

cryolite   chemical compound containing sodium, aluminium, and fluorine (sodium hexafluoro aluminate or sodium aluminium fluoride)

dynamo   type of electric generator that produces DC (direct current) electricity

electrode   one of the two poles of an electrical cell (battery)

electrolysis   making chemical reactions happen in a substance by passing electricity through it

electron   tiny, electrically-charged particle that is part of an atom. An electron has a negative charge.

element   simple substance that contains only one kind of atom

fuel cell   power source that produces electricity like a battery, but runs on fuel (usually hydrogen or methane)

generator   machine that makes electricity

hybrid   (in vehicles) vehicle that has an electric motor for slower driving and a petrol or diesel engine that cuts in when more power is needed

hydride   chemical compound in which a metal is combined with hydrogen

hydroelectric   generation of electricity from the energy derived from water

induction   process by which an electric current is produced in a wire moving in a magnetic field, or in a stationary wire in a changing magnetic field

insulator   material that does not allow electricity to pass through it easily

ion   atom that is electrically charged

kinetic energy   energy of movement

lithium   soft metal that is less dense than water

manganese   grey-white metal that is similar to iron but harder and more brittle

mercury   silver-grey metal that exists as a liquid at room temperature

MRI   magnetic resonance imaging magnets are powerful superconducting magnets used in MRI scanners to provide internal pictures of a patient's body

ore   rock that is rich in metal or other valuable mineral

rotor   part of an electric motor or generator that spins round

semiconductor device   electronic component (part) made from silicon and other semiconductor materials

stator   part of an electric motor or generator that does not rotate

superconductor   material that has no electrical resistance

transformer   electrical device that can change the voltage of an AC power source

turbine   type of fan or propeller that rotates in a moving stream of liquid or gas

Van de Graaff generator   machine that can generate very high electrical charges

Index